NO FOOL LIKE AN OLD FOOL

By the same author

POEMS AND SONGS
(Fortune Press)

LONDONERS
(Heinemann)

PLEASURES OF THE FLESH
(Alan Ross)

THE DECEPTIVE GRIN OF THE GRAVEL
PORTERS
(London Magazine Editions)

THE GAVIN EWART SHOW
(Trigram Press)

BE MY GUEST!
(Trigram Press)

PENGUIN MODERN POETS No. 25
(with Zulfikar Ghose and B. S. Johnson)

NO FOOL LIKE AN OLD FOOL

POEMS

by

GAVIN EWART

LONDON . VICTOR GOLLANCZ LTD . 1976

ACKNOWLEDGEMENTS

A proportion of these poems have appeared in the following periodicals and radio programmes: *Ambit, Encounter, Gallery, The Honest Ulsterman, The Listener, London Magazine, New Poetry I,* the Arts Council anthology, *The New Review, The New Statesman, Outposts,* George MacBeth's *Poetry Now* (B.B.C. 3), and in the *Poetry Supplement* of the Poetry Book Society, Christmas 1974, compiled by Philip Larkin.
Some have also been read on the Greater London Arts Association's Dial-a-Poem service.

PRINTED IN GREAT BRITAIN
BY EBENEZER BAYLIS AND SON LIMITED
THE TRINITY PRESS, WORCESTER, AND LONDON

CONTENTS

Part Three: The So-Called Sonnets

AN EXTENDED APOSTROPHE TO
JOHN HATCH CLARK, A COMRADE BOTH
ANCIENT AND MODERN

Dear CLARK, the Name on which I build,
My Shield and Hiding Place,
Whose Promise was not unfulfill'd,
Intelligence and Grace

Abounding greatly even then
In Nineteen-Thirty-Five
When in your Sojourn among Men
I first saw you alive,

The Master of the Cricket Bat,
The Cut and Legside Flick,
Adorn'd by Scholar's Gown and Hat—
As by a double Wick

You burn'd the Candle at both Ends,
With Sport and Intellect
Astonishing your many Friends
Of ev'ry Creed and Sect,

Fair OXFORD's ambidext'rous Pride,
In each Hand a fair Torch
The Way t'illuminate, and guide
With Flame that would not scorch

But show a calm and mod'rate Light
Upon the Way Ahead
To that imagin'd distant bright
Pavilion of the Dead,

Where those who gain a First in Greats,
And those who score the Goals,
Alike submit to those three Fates,
While those who frisked like Foals

Lie down at last t'Eternal Rest
And, feeling rather tired,
We too shall sleep, O brave and best,
O CLARK, my much-admired!

Part One

PROFESSOR OTTO LIDENBROCK TO WYSTAN HUGH AUDEN

(as of 29th September, 1974)

You were a rare one indeed—
in crabbed Runic letters from Iceland
you put your message across

early, when Terror abroad
demanded the bardic responses.
Arne Saknussem alas!

with his alchemical lore
could never have flummoxed the Axis;
Snorro Turleson too once

wrote of the foreigner's rule,
a country so banjaxed by Norway.
Gehlenites, fangasites still

(walking-on parts, without speech)
and our titanite of zirconium,
minerals both of us loved,

neutral, embellish the stage.
That's why we now hold them, inhuman,
in unregenerate hands;

we change much faster than they,
and people have called rocks eternal.
You, by one year, are diffuse.

I saw the light of my day
one hundred and ten years ago now,
    yes, quite eccentric and odd,

    much given to anger; they said
my sharp nose attracted iron filings—
    students don't have much respect.

    Diesel and Daimler and Benz
by no means had caused the commotion
    later you found so ungay—

    skies were for poets and birds,
our roads weren't as straight but quite fumeless,
    beam engines still were around.

    That was the so-simple scene
that one could call Middle Industrial.
    You'd have been happy, I know,

    in that mechanical peace
before we had jet-lag and nylon.
    Odd you most certainly were,

    not one to welcome the brash
insensitive probe of the bedroom;
    I was a funny one too.

    Liking to think that we share
a true geological mania,
    comrade, I send you my peace!

NOTE: In Jules Verne's *Journey To The Centre Of The Earth* (1864), Professor
Lidenbrock is the Leader of the expedition.

A DOUBLE VIEW

'If you will but speak the word, I will make you a good syllabub of new verjuice: and then you may sit down in a haycock, and eat it; and Maudlin shall sit by and sing you the good old song of the "Hunting in Chevy Chase" . . . '—Izaak Walton, THE *COMPLEAT ANGLER*, 1652.

'I only want men with really enormous pricks—nine inches and more. . . . Just imagine what I could do to a prick that long! I could lash it to a miniature whipping post and then flagellate it with tiny, jewel-handled whips.'—Joan C., Sunderland. Letter in *CLUB INTERNATIONAL*, 1974.

Relax. Don't get high blood pressure
for rural or Merrie England.
There are many different kinds of pleasure,
they could even mingle and
be none the worse;
nor is one really the reverse

of the other. Bees are humming,
all right, in the warm heather . . .
but you've got another think coming
if you think that was altogether
a Golden Age;
Civil War was all the rage

when Walton put Piscator in this idyll,
and whipping posts were real,
witnesses tortured, in the very middle
of a century ideal
only to us;
who make sentimental fuss

about the Past (past enough, and done with,
we love it!). A good time is
the choice of whom or what you have fun with;
for example, Yanks and Limeys
might not agree.
In the year 1653,

when Cromwell was proclaimed Lord Protector,
a man like staunch Venator,
if you got at him with a lie detector,
would be found a masturbator
as like as not;
only the very greatest clot

thinks that the fantasy worlds are wicked
(the staff might write the letters?),
mild sadomasochism isn't cricket.
Elders aren't always betters—
and an excuse
for *not* eating verjuice

(such a dreamy word) would be most necessary—
since unripe grapes/apples were ingredients.
Also, the letter-writer's accessory
jewel-handled whips are expedients
full of style;
imagination! better by a mile

than the rack, and the crude pressing
to death that was actual.
Rustic peace seems window-dressing.
Though, if we're being factual,
it appears
we've not changed much in three hundred years.

THE THEORY OF THE LEISURE CLASS

In those huge Victorian novels that were written during the
  time when Tennyson was occupied with Marianas and Mauds
people were saying things like 'What do you think, my
                            dear sir, in general, of pious frauds?'
and the language was pompous in the extreme and you might
        guess they one and all were as cold-blooded as saurians;
though we know now they all had Secret Lives and
      were having a high old time with those Other Victorians.

There were *malades imaginaires* and interesting invalids
              and ladies with permanently weakened constitutions,
while the rough gin-drinking populace starved or
                      enjoyed themselves at public executions.
The ambition of the wealthy was, quite seriously, to do
      absolutely nothing but to drink, to ride, to dance, to flirt.
Gambling for high stakes, soldiering, politics, the
                        buying of a new horse or a new skirt.

These were the only approved interests. Making money was
            trade. It must have been very gentlemanly but boring,
especially for the ladies, who weren't allowed—
      like their husbands and boy friends—to go off whoring.
Governesses suffered most. They had to be well-behaved
                  examples and quite preternaturally respectable.
They couldn't get drunk or encourage (or satisfy
            the desires of) men, however delectable.

In a hundred years or so we've changed, with our haircuts
            and our democratic adolescents in classless clothes,
though those with the wealth don't show many signs of
                        being terribly different from those

whose motto (What We Have We Hold) they held—as
        Mr. Mantalini might say—'like some demd vempire',
and our commercial predominance hasn't survived
                two wars and the disposal of an Empire.

Almost every class now is a leisure class, occupied (as
        it might be) with The Who, The Beatles or Bingo,
turned on by the telly, passively entertained by
              electronic football, Ken Russell, Ringo.
It all makes one think of bread and circuses, of
        those century-gone lives idle and under a blight;
how William Morris, who wanted handicrafts instead
        of machines, might very well have been right.

INCIDENT, SECOND WORLD WAR
(*In Memoriam P. M. B. Matson*)

It was near the beginning of that war. 1940 or '41,
when everything was fairly new to almost everyone.
The bombing of cities we understood, and blackouts; and
                      certainly, thanks
to the German Army and Air Force, we'd seen dive-bombers
                      and tanks.
But when the fighters came in to strafe with
                hedge-hopping low attacks
how many bits and pieces would be picked up to fill the sacks?
Aircraft cannon were not much fun for the weary
                  grounded troops
and there wasn't much entertainment when the
               Stukas were looping loops
but nobody knew for certain the percentage who
                 wouldn't get up,
how many would be donating their arms or their legs to Krupp.
So somebody in an office had the very bright idea,
why not set up an Exercise: machine-gunning from the air?
The War Office would know exactly the kind of
                figures involved,
an exciting statistical problem could be regarded as solved.

In a field, they put khaki dummies, on the reverse
                side of a hill.
And afterwards, they reckoned, they could estimate the kill.
Opposite these was the audience, to watch the total effect,
a sort of firework display—but free—the RAF being
                the architect.
All arms were represented? I think so. A grandstand seat
was reserved for top brass and others, a healthy
               open air treat;

enclosed, beyond the dummies, they stood (or sat?)

                                   and smoked
or otherwise passed the time of day, relaxed as they

                                talked and joked.

An experienced Spitfire pilot was briefed to fly over low
and give those dummies all he'd got—the star turn of

                                  the show,
with all the verisimilitude of a surprise attack.
Then to his fighter station he would whizz round and back.
They waited. And suddenly, waiting, they saw that

                                angel of death
come at them over the hillside. Before they could draw breath
he passed with all guns firing; some fell on their faces, flat,
but the benefit was minimal that anyone had from that.
He reckoned that *they* were the dummies, in his

                         slap-happy lone-wolf way,
that trigger-crazy pilot. He might have been right, some say.
But bitterness and flippancy don't compensate for men's lives
and official notifications posted to mothers and wives.

Nevertheless, there *were* results; percentages were

                                 worked out,
how 10 per cent could be written off, the wounded

                               would be about
50 per cent or so. Oh yes, they got their figures all right.
Circulated to units. So at least that ill-omened flight
was a part of the Allied war effort, and on the credit side—
except for those poor buggers who just stood there and died.

ENDING

The love we thought would never stop
now cools like a congealing chop.
The kisses that were hot as curry
are bird-pecks taken in a hurry.
The hands that held electric charges
now lie inert as four moored barges.
The feet that ran to meet a date
are running slow and running late.
The eyes that shone and seldom shut
are victims of a power cut.
The parts that then transmitted joy
are now reserved and cold and coy.
Romance, expected once to stay,
has left a note saying GONE AWAY.

RAIN—NO PLAY

Poem written instead of going to Lord's (a famous cricket ground)

Some tall and typical English Awfuls
were flowering outside the Royal Academy
buttonholed in the suits of tailors,
male and female and like stick insects,
from the top of a surging bus I saw them
in a sort of Vision of Piers the Plowman.

Well-turned-out were the waisted women,
of the kind that once at cocktail parties
wore hats and gloves and sipped their sherry,
the men were wonderful in their waistcoats.
A Summer Exhibition they themselves were,
as perfumed and orderly as an English garden.

Lords and Ladies of a small Creation,
noteworthy for having lots of money,
there they stood in the grey May weather
with cigarettes in 'amusing' holders
reminding of the Twenties, their bygone heyday—
and made intellectuals feel self-righteous.

Such people still in a sense are powerful
(some are witty and many charming),
wealth and property must still be reckoned with
in this very beautiful backward country
which one wouldn't swap for regimes of Europe
or the picturesqueness of all the peasants.

Though they don't like Art, these took the trouble
at least to look at those daubs, official
representatives of a past Old Order—
they don't reckon Art much in the Buildings,
it squeezes in sideways on the telly.
Philistia has a classless society.

Patronage was part of that once tradition,
we should never forget what we owe to idiots
who provided cash for the private building—
and not all, naturally, were all that silly
though their descendants look a bit blighted
planted out in this other Eden.

They wander now like the dead in Homer,
pallid ghosts who once were warriors,
still follow patterns, the prides of prep schools,
but as a class they are on their uppers
in a Britain that has heard of social justice
like a dark rumour in black-suited boardrooms.

The rain streams down, and the vision's fading.
Who will understand this precarious phenomenon
(in a London where, like Mother Church, stood Harrods,
centre of pilgrimage) in another century?
The cricket fields are stretched out green and useless,
they too survivals of a Past not perfect.

POETS

It isn't a very big cake,
some of us won't get a slice,
and that, make no mistake,
can make us not very nice
to one and all—or another
poetical sister or brother.

We all want total praise
for every word we write,
not for a singular phrase;
we're ready to turn and bite
the thick malicious reviewers,
our hated and feared pursuers.

We feel a sad neglect
when people don't buy our books;
it isn't what we expect
and gives rise to dirty looks
at a public whose addiction
is mainly romantic fiction.

We think there's something wrong
with poets that readers *read*,
disdaining our soulful song
for some pretentious screed
or poems pure and simple
as beauty's deluding dimple.

We can't imagine how
portentous nonsense by A
is loved like a sacred cow,
while dons are carried away

by B's more rustic stanzas
and C's banal bonanzas.

We have our minority view
and a sort of trust in Time;
meanwhile in this human zoo
we wander free, or rhyme,
our admirers not very many—
lucky, perhaps, to have any.

YORKSHIREMEN IN PUB GARDENS

As they sit there, happily drinking,
their strokes, cancers and so forth are not in their minds.
    Indeed, what earthly good would thinking
about the future (which is Death) do? Each summer finds
    beer in their hands in big pint glasses.
    And so their leisure passes.

Perhaps the older ones allow some inkling
into their thoughts. Being hauled, as a kid, upstairs to bed
    screaming for a teddy or a tinkling
musical box, against their will. Each Joe or Fred
    wants longer with the life and lasses.
    And so their time passes.

Second childhood; and 'Come in, number 80!'
shouts inexorably the man in charge of the boating pool.
    When you're called you must go, matey,
so don't complain, keep it all calm and cool,
    there's masses of time yet, masses, masses . . .
    And so their life passes.

ADOLESCENT AGONIES

Though my potential is enormous
examinations give me traumas,
and women with their little pee-things,
chattering among the tea things.
Self, oh, self! Oh, thou that kissest
the upturned face of this narcissist!
All my thoughts, directed mewards,
miss the glories that lie seawards,
my psyche is in such a panic
I can't start feeling oceanic.

Venus with her pouting bust is
no consoler for injustice,
everywhere the poor are treated
like phrases that must be deleted.
It makes me feel I'm going barmy
to see how often it's an Army
that rules the young illiberal countries.
O Diana, Queen and Huntress,
moonlike maid with circling crescent,
have pity on this adolescent!

We are nothing, we are zeros,
completely in the power of Eros,
here to-day and gone to-morrow,
in a vale of tears and sorrow,
in a time of crime and crisis
licking lollies, eating ices.
When the social groups first started
were men even then cold-hearted?
Did we never care for others?
What's that archaic word now? 'Brothers'?

I reject what admen taught us,
I reject the plays of Plautus,
classical and other studies,
the conmen and the fuddy-duddies.
Both are very far from noble.
My distress is yours—and global.
I am Man, not very happy
in the nightie or the nappy,
not enjoying his sins and sexes,
husbands, wives or sorrowing exes.

You can't ignore my wounded feelings
in your Exeters and Ealings,
mine is trouble that surpasses
differences of clocks and classes;
though you are completely gormless
and your life is calm and stormless,
hire purchase mortgage man, flat-renter,
I live at the stormy centre.
I am in that sad condition:
permanently in transition.

YEATS AND SHAKESPEARE

Somebody wrote somewhere (about Yeats)
how even in those wasp-waisted days
before the First World War
(for twenty years reckoned among the Greats)
he was so spoiled by worship and by praise
he couldn't behave naturally any more,

as hostesses crept up behind his back
with every kind of social, sexual net
and pecking order snare;
a lion with hyenas on his track
or hunters closing in, they say, and yet
he never seemed to find this hard to bear.

Shakespeare was not so honoured in his life
though (for a player) he ended rich,
great ladies didn't swoon
to hear or see him; and a bitter wife,
it is presumed, told him the what and which
of all his faults, and told him pretty soon.

Arnold was John the Baptist, coming late
to smooth the way for universal awe,
but one thing he got right:
Shakespeare was lucky not to be thought great
outside the Mermaid, or above the law.
It's best for geniuses to travel light.

THE ARGUMENT FOR
THE BENEVOLENT GOD

Suppose a sadist,
after keeping a most beautiful woman in strict bondage for
a year, with occasional beatings and other indignities, living
shall we say in some decadent Egypt, Durrellian and impure,
suppose he at the end of this time caused her to be locked
into a special appliance, a mummiform case of stainless
steel, exactly tailored to her mouth-watering measurements,
with a headpiece like the mask worn by fencers, allowing
her to see, hear and speak—but not to move. Suppose only
from this smooth impervious steel casing her two
well-nourished breasts, like soft hills, protruded, pink
and unprotected. Suppose then this sadist caused her to
be transported deep into lion country and, in spite of
her weeping, while the lazy sly attendants pinched her
nipples, left her there; while he watched from a
luxurious hide, drinking Johnnie Walker, until a big
brazen lion happened along, his great yellow balls
like puffballs at the point of bursting, sniffed,
cautiously approached and pawed her, screaming. Suppose
finally he tore the breasts and bit them, ate them down
as far as his muzzle allowed, blood on stainless steel,
murder and mayhem . . .

Suppose a deity,
after making as the legends claim a delectable woman
from the hard rib of a man, but making her soft and
nubile and adapted to child-bearing, and after the
love affairs and the kissing, the raising of skirts
and the sexual adoration, in trains, on kitchen tables,
in borrowed flats, in cornfields, in woodlands full of
rabbits; if after all this sincere worship of the spirit

of Procreation, he allowed procreation itself and
probably marriage, the infants pulling at the very much
publicised breasts, pink and unprotected. Suppose, with
the children in their teens or entirely grown up, the woman
still attractive found in one breast a small lump, which
was excised as a cancer. Suppose there was radiation
treatment but suppose just suppose that this deity arranged
it so that the cancer reached the bloodstream and appeared
(perhaps within a year) somewhere on the back perhaps or
the base of the spine, and after all the depression and
discomfort of the radiation, the tiredness and the hopelessness,
she sank into a long death, sedated in a silent scream,
oblivion washing over her, far from lion country but
martyred by motherhood . . .

HURRIED LOVE

Those who make hurried love don't do so
from any lack of affection
or because they despise their partner
as a human being—
what they're doing
is just as sincere as a more formal wooing.

She may have a train to catch; perhaps the
room is theirs for one hour only
or a mother is expected back or
some interruption
known, awaited—
so the spur of the moment must be celebrated.

Making love against time is really
the occupation of all lovers
and the clock-hands moving
point a moral:
not crude but clever
are those who grab what soon is gone for ever.

LAST MOVEMENTS

In Old Master music in sonata form,
by Mozart, by Schubert, you always find,
after the sadness and the emotional storm
that moves or maddens the listening mind,
strumming the nerves like the strings they play,
that four, five or six will make the mood gay.

This is a convention, we know, of course,
and a wistfulness in the rumti-ti-tum
might be detected; the sorrow's force
gives way to the logical musical sum,
as vigorously, brightly, the players bend
to a dance where unhappiness comes to an end.

But perhaps there's thanksgiving concealed there too
for a life that also contained some joy,
a kind of reminder for me and you
that nothing's pure, and without alloy
nothing. The dark swallows up despair
as well as hope—says that rustic air.

SWARM OVER, DEATH!

(Jannice Porter. Slough Crematorium. 20th December, 1974.)

The planes are roaring at Heathrow
like lions at a zoo,
above Stoke Poges, near and low,
whose churchyard holds a clue
to what it is we still don't know
and what we have to do.

Under the warm and leafless bough
of this pre-winter time
we zero in to dismal Slough
as witness to a crime—
departure from our here and now
of one no wit or rhyme

can possibly in joy recall
from that uncharted state.
If God's responsible for all
(unless you call him Fate)
he seems revengeful for that Fall
and neither soon nor late

his crematoria give up,
consolatory, a ghost.
Bitter for kids, a Kiddie Kup
prepared; like flaming toast,
a sudden flare, a quick kerflup!
mums vanish. At the most

hygienic, I suppose you'd say;
but for survivors sad,

who don't forget a better day
when Friendship made them glad,
Love and Affection came to stay
and a good time was had

by one and all. The words seem trite,
like brandnames, not inspired,
like golf balls simply called Kro-Flite
(imagination tired)
or Samuel watches: Ever-rite.
We are not lit or fired

by any mystic inner glow.
We envy, everywhere,
the animals who just don't know
or, if they know, don't care—
who go because they have to go
in face of Death's blank stare.

If all's ordained, as some will say,
(we start the little cars
and in our groups we drive away)
by God or by our stars,
it isn't very fair or gay
or arguable in bars.

LOOKING FOR BOOKS

In even the best library, looking through the poetry shelves
is a depressing experience for poets;
they might not expect to find *themselves*

but they don't find many of their contemporaries either.
Instead of MacBeth and Porter—Mrs. Wilson.
Slim volumes act elusive, hard to catch, lither

than lizards and the big fat books of critics
whose size and weight can often stun us.
Like aphasiacs or mental paralytics

Tennyson; The Critical Heritage by John D. Jump
knocks us out by just its title,
The Poems and Translations of Thomas Stanley ed.
                                        G. M. Crump

promises oceans of the greatest learnèd boredom
(unless the ridiculous names mislead us).
With these the Muse has not committed whoredom,

we suspect; they're innocent of her as Big Ears, Noddy
or Aneirin Talfan Davies,
author of *Dylan—Druid of the Broken Body*.

And, in general, Heavy Verse tends to come out on top,
serious *Crows*, the loud mystique of
self-congratulatory suicide. Light Verse must have a stop,

it seems, and only a continuous shrill hysteria
vary the pieces on voles and
large and small animals, the harebells, the wistaria

and every local landscape of the regional chauvinist.
Sad it may be, but one could say that
a fit epitaph ('They'll none of them be missed')

is already pronounced; and frailly Stevie Smith
resists Time with one *Selected Poems*.
The runaway actual factual leaves the myth

('Stevie Smith? Oh, yes, I like *him*!' a big beard said
gauche to me once at a poetry reading),
we are not even remembered, let alone read.

THE RETURN OF THE HERO

He overclomb cliffs   in that far country
With wolves and with water mains   he fought so freely
In briars and badgerdoms   he rabbited rebels
Swooningly swimming   the turnable tidemarks
Incredible crows   cratered the causeway
Dark were the doorways   with feral foxes
Energetic enemies   falsified his feebleness
Firm amid fire alarms   he prevented panic
Dragons and discotheques   peacefully pacified
In supermarkets   he limited looting
For his high heroics   the ladies were lusting
No one had seen such   baronial beauty
        Before.
His body was seemly and straight,
His height was as high as a door,
Waiting women couldn't wait,
They were asking for more.

Back from the beastliness   in haste he hurried
Never so knowingly   chroniclers charted him
Hazards of hell   on a fiery field
Gaping gestapos   ominously overtured
To borderline cases   he brought early warning
Charmingly championed   the softer sexes
In testified triumph   great bronze bells beat
Trumpets like tramlines   blazed in beaconry
Voices avowed him   charisma in chorus
In festive fountains   wine was wobbling
The boldest beauties   kowtowed with kissing
Opened their opulence   with liking unlimited
        By thought.

This was instinctive as praise,
No one could say it was bought,
They offered it all in a phrase,
And more than they ought.

Yet he, no knave,   as a good knight should
Was shunning their sherry   in crystal cups
Frowning at fathers   brandishing brandy
Slow to sly hints   from matchmaking mothers
Edging his eyes round   the bountiful bosoms
Never noticing   nubile necks
Counting as nothing   their see-through somethings
Solidly sober   among the amphetamines
Decidedly derisive   of their deliberate dancing
Regarding all praise   as pitiful prize money
And the randy rewards   of righteous restlessness
Not worth a worm-cast   and simply silly
        Or trite.
He kept his nose clean, you see,
He never refused out of fright,
He knew that, on land as on sea,
A wrong can't be right.

So did they sententiously   serenade his seemliness?
Praise his purity   in post-prandial prose?
Statue his stateliness   in exquisite squares?
Nibbling nasties   on the contrary
Combined to erode   his reputation
Hinting at horrors   of hired holography
Monsters mastered   by fallacious fixing
Elevated to epidemics   an only outbreak
Clouted and cloven   cardboard animals
Vintage volcanoes   firecracker falsies
No eager activity   but lazy legend

His asexual exploits   rendered as rat-poison
            Not good.
The moral is simple and sad:
The monk doesn't make the hood,
You're never untouched by what's bad
Or out of the wood.

THE ONE-TIME THREE-QUARTER
REMEMBERS THE PAST

Pulling on a clammy jersey from a prep school locker
and the boots with dry earth caked round leather studs
and after a defeat to hear the bitter précis
of the mad and shell-shocked master.

This was the game that I found more fun than soccer
and a bright day meant good running, with the ball
easy to handle, neither wet nor greasy;
wind distracting, mud disaster.

We came after a war where the terrifying word Fokker
embodied something as beastly as the opposing teams
we hated and feared; now we walk slowly,
it is time that moves much faster.

So on a bright morning we know, though age is a mocker,
that the afternoon's International will be played fast;
we run now in our minds only,
old chairs, with one loose caster.

Old family cars have a certain appeal.
Families get fond of them. Cartoonists
love to draw them with big round eyes.
Also, of course, in a way they are monsters—
like other pets, dogs in particular, they are polluters,
fuming up the high streets. They kill people.

All cars, too, are rooms on wheels; and have witnessed
acts of love, arguments, affectionate banter,
the behaviour of children. Like animals, like us,
they deteriorate with time. The earth renews
but they do not renew. A licence in April
brings no bright resurgence of power and beauty.

If you've been fond of one, it's hard to think of it
chained with battered others on the big transporter,
cracked windows, dented like a toy
by a termagant two-year-old; the words Old Faithful
come to mind to remind of the so many journeys.
Turner felt the same about the Fighting Téméraire.

THE SECOND COMING

I say the Sphinx was the Boston Strangler;
and He will be born again in Oklahoma
(I shall wear the feathers of the blue crane,
which are the mark of a great warrior)
and all over the campus the boys in sneakers
will do him peculiar acts of homage,
not forgetting the earlier avatar.

A sign will be seen in Anne Hathaway's cottage.
As I walked through the wilderness of this world
I knew He would be hatched from a hen's egg
with a preference for soils that are argillaceous
and a liking for hominy grits and grapefruit.
I put on pride as a kind of humbleness
to announce a new wonder among the libraries.

I shall purify myself in a kraal or igloo,
refusing the offered breasts of the women,
it's all in the small print in my contract,
microfilmed on my brain; and His Word is sacred.
On the third day I shall emerge to testify
a miraculous birth, for the Muse a boyfriend
and for us a new speech and a life-enhanced language.

THE ILLNESS OF THE WRITER'S WIFE

If you thought you were dying of cancer
you wouldn't give a civil answer;
and the best reviews that you could muster
wouldn't make very much difference, buster.

You might become a trifle moody,
although you're drinky, fat and foody,
if the future seemed so bloody
and there was no escaping, buddy.

You too would blaze up just as soon, ding-
donging words both harsh and wounding;
if you remember, pain's not funny
when it lasts a long time, sonny.

You could be Shakespeare or Homer,
threatened by a carcinoma
your life too'd be sad and weary—
your main desire survival, dearie.

For nursery days are gone, nightmare is
real and there are no Good Fairies.
The fox's teeth are in the bunny
and nothing can remove them, honey.

IS THERE LIFE AFTER SEX?

Sad old people are no longer nubile,
the fucate ladies have wrinkled faces,
the men can defy gravity no more now
than they can fly or accomplish bilocation
or levitate; the accustomed miracles
of hardness or wetness are past, long past.

This doesn't mean that they have no feeling;
inhabitants of an oblate spheroid,
they too were never completely perfect,
perhaps they never were drawn to bedrooms
to handle the contents of skirts or trousers,
what you've never had you can't miss.

But love survives and the fact of nearness,
too much sympathy may not be in order,
they may have enjoyed much more than we have;
touch is, after all, an animal comfort.
In a way, perhaps, the mind doesn't need it—
obmutescence is an answer too.

Leave the potency to the grandsons,
they could say and entirely mean it.
Love is more than florulent verbiage
and all delightful extravagant action
is simply tenderness as a double crown poster,
could be condensed to a postage stamp.

Eschatological serious theories
never mentioned the end of pleasure
or took cognisance of those organs
that can induce a secular ecstasy;

gave us a huge and sombre fresco,
no quick humanist esquisse.

If latinists are shouting *Cave canem*
there's life in the old dog yet, believe me,
beyond the false gods of procreation.
It's a great mistake, jampacked with error,
farctate with jumbo disappointments,
to make active sex a sacred cow.

Part Two

WILLIAM McGONAGALL ON
ENGLAND'S FAILURE TO QUALIFY
FOR THE WORLD CUP, 1974

Now that the English have discovered they're
                              on a sticky wicket
And their Test teams aren't as good as they thought
                              they were at cricket,
And they've now absolutely completely lost face
Even at football, what will the Nation do about this disgrace?
I think they ought all to swarm to the cliffs and
                              in communal despair
Throw themselves into the sea, in a noble mass
                              suicide darkening the air.

A PERSONAL FOOTNOTE

'In addition, he will give you seven women, skilled in the fine crafts, Lesbians whom he chose for their exceptional beauty . . .'
—THE ILIAD, Book 9.

Nobody has ever offered
to give me seven Lesbians—
though I was once a warrior
for six long years,
slept in a tent too
on a sparse camp bed.

Somehow I missed the
spoils of the cities.
I was not important.
A silly Lieutenant
can't sulk and get
away with it

like grandiose Achilles.

WILLIAM WORDSWORTH (1770–1850)

Most modern Nature Lovers have a personal scale of values
                that tells them what each tree, hill or bird's worth;
but this doesn't quite apply to Wordsworth.
For Wordsworth, as it were, believing was much the
                      same as seeing—
he thought natural phenomena were the guardians of
                  his heart and soul of all his moral being.
The meadows and the woods and mountains kept him on the
                    straight and narrow
when he felt like getting pissed in places like
                    Applethwaite or Yarrow.
If he had an urge to go out on a thrash
he would have to ask permission from a mountain ash.
Nature was a kind of ever-present Nurse
supervising all his life and all his verse.

The only time the system broke down seems to
                    have been in France
when he was young and revolutionary, and every advance
in progressive thought was welcome. He wasn't the
                  star of any leading lady's salon,
but he succeeded completely in seducing a girl
                  called Annette Vallon.
Though she became pregnant and had a B-A-B-Y
William by then had wandered off, lonely as a cloud in a
                  Lake District sky.
It all sounds very natural—but Nanny wasn't pleased;
there is absolutely no doubt at all that William was seized
by a fit of remorse and secrecy. From then on
                  no man was a brother
and he never again fancied republicanism or a bit of the other.

This, at any rate, is what they say. They say too that
                    mountains for him were father-figures
and wonderful things in his eyes, as wonderful as Tiggers.
But a more interesting question is *How did it come about?*
This wasn't exactly the first time that William
                              had been allowed out.
It sounds to me like a failure in communication, a
                              misunderstanding.
Perhaps French trees, like the French, were too
                    logical and not used to handing
out advice and instructions for people's love life or guidance
on what to do next, like the Athenes, Zeuses and Poseidons
who made Odysseus' life so difficult? Was William *en rapport*
with the French meadows, woods, etc? Or did they say
                                   'Tu as tort!'
when he told them they ought to be guardians of
                              his moral being,
and chuckle in a Gallic way? Or just start *oui, oui*-ing?
I think he would have avoided all that guilt and loss if he
had managed to give himself a less ridiculous philosophy.

THE CRICKET OF MY FRIENDS

Ross in his days of youth
was quite a bowler,
energy rushed through his veins
like Coca-Cola,

he could concentrate like an obsessive
loony from Rampton,
he certainly played for Oxford
and for Northampton.

Worsley was another natural
born for cricket—
in the Cambridge University team
he once kept wicket.

Clark, with a bat in his hand,
could show his talents,
his timing and footwork were good
and so was his balance.

Symons could play a bit,
though table tennis
was the game where he made his mark
as a national menace

and worked himself up to be
reserve for England—
though never as good as the Chinks
from ping-pong Ming land.

Romilly, Rycroft and Madge
couldn't play for toffee—

they were fonder of sitting and talking
and drinking coffee.

I can't imagine a century
being made by Spender.
Was Fuller ever more
than a good tail-ender?

(I may be doing him a real
savage injustice).
Connolly—an acquaintance—
was better at pastis.

At least this is my own piece
of intelligent guesswork.
There's a gap between bat and pad
and playing and press work.

You can't see Angus Wilson
driving firmly through the covers;
the literary ladies
prefer playing games with lovers.

It's sad to see how little
the literati
have really achieved at cricket—
though hale and hearty

they don't seem to have the *flair*.
The French are hopeless.
If clean cricket were next to godliness
they would be soapless.

So it's all a bad business—
like the murder of a Kennedy—
as for Literary Cricket
I offer up this threnody.

A VERY SHOCKING POEM
FOUND AMONG THE PAPERS OF
AN EMINENT VICTORIAN DIVINE

I saw you with Septimus on the parterre
    In front of the old Bishop's Palace.
The sunshine was weaving its gold in your hair
    But my heart was embittered and malice
Moved in me mightily; jealous was I
    And I burned with desire to distress you,
To down-thunder like Jove from that clear summer sky
    And at once, then and there, to undress you!

That hand, once in mine, was in his as you walked
    And answered him in your bright treble;
Not a word could I hear but I knew that you talked
    And the Flesh rose up like a dark rebel—
For that hand, as I knew, was an adjunct to Love,
    Like a hot caper sauce to hot mutton,
And designed by the Lord to descend from above
    First to fondle—and then to unbutton!

Ah! those feet that ran to me won't run to me now,
    The dismal and desperate fact is
They will turn to avoid me, for you will know how
    To go home with the Choir after Practice—
Though you lingered once sweetly to dally with me
    And our preoccupations weren't choral
As you sat in the sitting-room there on my knee
    And the examination was oral!

I saw those eyes opening, gazing at him
    With the blue of the midsummer heaven,
My own eyes with traitorous tear-drops grew dim

And of Rage, lustful Rage, a black leaven
Worked in me there; for those eyes once had seen
    (Thought to break my heart, break it and rive it)
On the ottoman, proud in its velvety green,
    Those parts that our God has called private!

I dream of a Paradise still, now and then,
    But it is not the orthodox milieu
Where good spirits abound—with no women or men.
    Ah! My Conscience lies drowned like Ophelia!
And my Heaven's a dream of an opulent South
    With soft cushions, wine, perfumes, bells ringing,
My member for ever held tight in your mouth
    And a thousand bright choirboys all singing!

LIMERICKS

Limericks are a serious thing
and as long as a short piece of string
with a sting in their tails,
unrestrainedly males,
and as wild as a wasp on the wing.

Some limericks never wash clean,
from their heads to their toes they're obscene;
though it's not these extremes
that elicit the screams
but the things that they've got in between.

They have oomph and some razamatazz,
they're as joky and jaunty as jazz,
they do far more than flirt,
they get under a skirt,
and defy all the Omo and Daz.

They're as epigrammatic as efts
and too slight to cause literary thefts—
for what author would steal
what's not even a meal
but a weed growing in crannies and clefts?

You can see them exploding like squibs,
untruthful and too fond of fibs,
crude, simple, and yet
one won't do as a pet—
they're not angels or babies in bibs.

It's their content, so beastly and bland,
that a Holbrook or Whitehouse can't stand.

If you hear one at night
it's much best to take fright
and retreat to your bed out of hand.

Though they seem unaccountably mild
don't let them get near to your child—
they can harm Mums and Dads
and all sensitive lads
come out coarsened and worsened and wild.

So study the Classical modes,
keep to elegies, epics and odes,
for their lewd beck and nod
is unwelcome to God
and traumatic as ten-fingered toads.

THE BLURB

This tenderly observant poet writes clearly,
rhythmically and thoughtfully,
about what all of us can understand . . .
This unperturbed, unenvious and compassionate
poet of doubt, common experience and
the search for truth, we ought fully
to appreciate . . .

He has a reverence for the vastness around us
and stands on the brink of eternity
wondering whether it will be day, twilight
or night when we are dead. He is the John Clare
of the building estates, true and right
to them as Clare to field and tree
and ploughshare . . .

He has certainly closed the gap between
poetry and the public which frankly
the experiments and obscurity of the last
fifty years have done so much (alas!) to widen . . .
he has a vibrant sense of our shared past,
of the *rerum* and their *lacrimae*,
dead Tyre and Sidon . . .

TO LORD BYRON

on the occasion of the 150th Anniversary of his death,
commemorated at the Victoria and Albert Museum

You didn't much like relics. The 'lying bust'
    seemed to you too impersonal and cold
to represent warm flesh, whose love and lust
    even the Puritans share (when not too old)
before they crumble into decent dust.
    What would *you* think of this? Would you feel 'sold'?
For geniuses, alas, it's a tradition
to end up as a paying Exhibition.

So here are portraits of that gang you banged,
    the bright, unstable, intellectual ladies;
evidence that an ancestor was nearly hanged
    (to roam, unblessed, the further shores of Hades),
that in the Lords you once stood and harangued
    and kept a bear at Cambridge. A bill (paid?) is
exhibited as proof (bear food and lodging)—
though, through your life, your debts were not for dodging.

Here, from Miss Chaworth to La Guiccioli,
    with delicate miniatures and locks of hair,
are philosophical ladies, prophetic, Nietzschely,
    high-waisted with their bosoms raised and bare—
but also bakers' wives, untamed, unteacherly,
    one that was married to a gondolier.
That auburn curl (for some peculiar reason)
of Lady Caroline Lamb gave me a *frisson*.

Pathetic, too, to read Allegra's letters
    in copybook Italian, guided by nuns,

who went to join her elders and her betters
    under those feverish Mediterranean suns
at five years old. *Caro Papa*. Hounds, setters,
    horses you kept. Children were shunned like duns.
Shelley, a guest at your Venetian palace,
was right to be angry and to call you callous.

But who am I to take a stance that's moral?
    Your entourage was not for little girls.
In any case it's far too late to quarrel—
    you were worth fifty of *our* Lords and Earls,
in days when atom bombs shake ocean coral
    we are the swine to whom you cast your pearls,
you stand like some far-shining distant lighthouse.
And what would you have thought of Mrs. Whitehouse?

Would you be keen on Peter Pan and Wendy
    or anything that's cosy, coy or twee?
Contrariwise, would you admire what's trendy
    (you were a fashion once yourself) or see
virtue in what's suburban or weekendy?
    To you, who only knew one kind of tea,
who never knew what roaches or a jag meant,
I dedicate this small Byronic fragment.

VALEDICTION: TO THE CRICKET SEASON

As a boy who has lost a girl so sadly
tears up a photograph or her early letters,
knowing that what has gone is gone for ever,
  a lustful bustful,

the exchange of confidences, the hours of cuddling,
the paraphernalia of what some call sharing,
so we mourn you; televisually prepare for
  their filthy football,

professional fouls and the late late tackle,
breakaway forwards held back by a jersey,
the winning or losing almost equally nasty.
  The English summer

is never perfect, but you are a feature
as pleasing to us as a day of sunshine,
to spectators at least a calm, straw-hatted
  Edwardian dandy.

Not really a game of physical contact,
the batsman pardons the ungentlemanly bouncer,
the only foul would be leg theory,
  bodyline bowling;

as nostalgic as those old school stories
the plock of bat on ball penetrates outfields,
calming to the mind. Warm pints of bitter
  and county cricket

are long married in our friendly folklore
of white marquees, the spires of cathedrals,

pitch-wandering dogs, boys on the boundary,
        mystified girlfriends,

all of it as much a myth and a ritual
as the fairy stories written by learned
elf-haunted dons who invent a cosmos
        neat but escapist,

where the rules are forever, can never be broken,
and a dragon, as it were, can be l.b.w.
if he puts a foot the wrong side of the mountain.
        You are the bright one

that shines in the memory; as old-fashioned writers
say 'she was a maid of some seventeen summers',
we don't reckon age by the passing of winters,
        by happier seasons

we count up that final inescapable total,
remember huge sixes by maverick sloggers—
compensating, like love, for the field that's deserted,
        the padlocked pavilion.

Part Three

THE SO-CALLED SONNETS

SONNET:
THE KNOWLEDGE OF GOOD AND EVIL

In the Twenties we had children's books that made
value judgments on wildlife, of an anthropomorphical kind:
The Hundred Best Animals, *Queer Fish* and *Secrets of the Zoo*.
Not to mention the way the Flopsy Bunnies ran into trouble.
But now when you read a novel about rabbits
it actually tells you the way rabbits live—
as far as anyone who is not a rabbit can work it out.
We've been told more, and we ought to know more.

But knowledge isn't enough. People have said
that Hitler immunized us against his myxomatosis for ever.
Yet an understanding of sadism doesn't prevent it.
So we have the Moors Murders, summary executions,
the torture of prisoners—so many little fascist states where
Hitler would be happy. You must want, as well as know.

SONNET: MOTHER LOVE

Women are always fond of growing things.
They like gardening; snipping, watering, pruning,
bringing on the backward, aware of the forward;
planting—not for nothing do they talk of 'nurseries'.
Roses are like children, a source of pride,
tulips are cosseted, primulas are pets.
These are almost as loved as the usual surrogates—
the dogs and cats that stand for families.

Conservation, preservation; it's a lovable aspect
of maternalism (one reason why we're here).
Better than that, this severe matriarchy
is established over *plants*; the bossiness, thank God,
that puts you there (delphiniums), you there (wallflowers),
is harmlessly deflected well away from us.

SONNET: MALTHUSIAN

All these wars, revolutions, famines, earthquakes, floods
are blessings—and not in disguise. They limit
the numbers of those who pollute the earth, a planet
growing colder to the greed of human life.
The Catholic exhortations to outnumbering
are, in our context, disastrously sectarian.
We ought to be far fewer. A general hope
attaches to circling nuclear devices.

Nobody wants to be, however, there—
on the particular spot of weeding out:
Palestine, Belfast, Uganda. Or to starve
with Africans and Asians. And that terrible **bomb**
would solve the problem too efficiently.
Smug doomwatchers, we keep the telly tuned.

SONNET: RED IN TOOTH AND CLAW

'Isn't Nature wonderful?' says a wondering lady
while a TV feature shows the cuteness of hedgehogs,
but can't look when a bustard is fed with a live mouse
and the snuffling hedgehog crunches a baby vole.
This is the Life people say they're on the side of—
and there's eating and being eaten in many a boardroom,
people too will kill to obtain food and status,
literally. For that, too, watch television.

One can see how the writers of all those little poems
celebrating wildlife, landscape and birdsong,
might set their faces against brutalism in concrete,
dreaming of that impossible, perfect, Rural England.
But 'brutal' and 'bestial' are words that come from animals:
foxes, to chickens, don't seem beautiful.

SONNET: CARSON McCULLERS

To go into your South, a different life.
Sowbelly and cornbread with syrup poured over it;
or fried slices of side meat, collard greens, hoecakes.
To go back and away towards the lonely freaks
who can't communicate, who never communicate,
and live on that diet of misunderstanding—
poor whites, poor blacks, who never get the message.
And what, for that matter, would ever be the message?

We all are freakish, mutes with hand signals;
even the most talkative outgoing lady
tells more about herself than what is actual.
Like the hot Italian *Mezzogiorno*
your country was richest in superstition.
Where you were a one-eyed person, they were blind.

SONNET: BEAR THOUGHTS

Like Sir John Betjeman, I too have a teddy bear—
from 1916 or thereabouts.
He sits in the hall, his fur rubbed through in places,
one eye a proper one, the other just a button
of a not very suitable kind. He wears my son's school cap
(discarded) and a shirt and shorts
made for him by my sisters years ago.
He looks worn, like a man of nearly fifty-nine.

I never talk to him. My daughter does.
I can't remember much of our early days;
this is a dead friendship and a long-past love.
What does survive (and witness Betjeman)
is a feeling that he indeed is truly living.
Probably no one completely outgrows his childhood.

SONNET: ONE

Where did *one* come from?
One is continually appalled by . . .
One feels that in this movement Monteverdi . . .
It must have been from the French (the Germans say *man*)
but when and where? Voltaire doesn't use it—
or does he? Nor the English (this is guesswork)
much before Henry James. I have a vision of aesthetes
leaning on Nineties mantelpieces, saying 'One . . . '

by which they mean 'I' much more than 'we'.
Critics and reviewers use it, but it's sideways-sliding;
it's better to say 'we' for a general judgment.
Critics can't be everybody, their omnience is fiction.
Nobody can ever speak for anybody but himself—
and even then in doubt and great confusion.

SONNET: MAD NATURE

The early morning crows are crowing all through
Wordsworth's famous *Ode To A Shylock*,
making a dull plonking sound like a bass guitar;
some sheep are singing a well-known chorus from *The Messiah*
about navigation—'All we like ships have gone astray'.
The soda fountains with their purling streams
bring transcendental music to the soul.
Park attendants shout a battle-cry: *Rus in urbe!*

Even if all this were so, it wouldn't be relevant
really to men in their expanding cities.
What we've lost, we've lost. And how far back
do you want to go? The wheelwright's shop? The Iron Age?
That noble anthropoid lived, not in innocence
but fighting with his wits, the same as us.

SONNET: TIDYING UP

Left lying about in my mind, awaiting collection,
are the thoughts and phrases that are quite unsuitable
and often shocking to all Right-thinking people—
penetrated by a purple penis for example
(almost a line?); and how it's almost certain,
from Swift's hints, that the big sexy ladies of Brobdingnag
used Gulliver as an instrument of masturbation.
Hence a tongue-twister: *Glumdalclitch's clitoris.*

Though not always decorous, there's a lot of force in phrases.
A good many poems stem from them; they start something.
More than anything Shakespeare owes his power to them
(his *secret, black and midnight hags* and hundreds more),
they almost consoled him—though life is pretty bloody
(*the multitudinous seas incarnadine*).

SONNET: NASTY

Never forget that everybody's nasty.
People can smile and pretend to be kind; it's
as often as not a façade, behind is a good deal of
selfishness and malevolence—which quickly become overt
at the quick flare of passion—then, behind the curtains
in that well-regulated villa, you see the torture-chamber.
Angel in the street, devil in the home. A saying.
Some are even devils in the home *and* devils in the street.

All this being so, my considered advice is:
always give everyone the benefit of the doubt,
consider them nice until proved otherwise.
But don't be too naive. The neighbours whose house is
continually filled with the screams of children
may say 'Hello!'—but 'nice' is not their adjective.

SONNET: THE PRIZE

The Prize is eternal peace. All sentient beings win it.
God, like a visiting celebrity, hands it to each
in a full convocation of everybody living,
the Pope or some magnified Prophet is there as Headmaster,
Housemasters are heads of the Sects, benevolent smilers
at a kind of never-ending award-giving Speech Day.
Do the animals get in on the act? Some people have thought so,
imagining cat Heavens, Purgatories for dogs . . .

This is what they say. Personally I think we do,
you and I and the ants in the ant-hill,
achieve eternal peace in our separate endings;
it's certain indeed nobody can bother us.
For those under pressure it sounds like a blessing—
except that we're no longer conscious to enjoy it.

SONNET: SENILITY

Go into a corner with a bottle of whisky
and grow old gracefully. Those are my
instructions to myself. In one of his essays
Montaigne says how in childhood
most life is concentrated in the extremities
(all that running, jumping, catching, throwing),
in the middle part of life—well, in the middle
(the active organs of romantic love).

This lasts well into old age. Life just moves up the body.
It lodges finally in the head and throat.
Long live golosity and intellect! Our food no longer
the food of love (though feminists, no-ball snowballs,
call every man a two-ball screwball, in pure disdain),
we can still eat and drink, and eat and drink . . .